Pitcher

Pitcher

George Sullivan

illustrated with photographs by the author

and line drawings by

Don Madden

Thomas Y. Crowell   New York

Text copyright © 1986 by George Sullivan
Illustrations copyright © 1986 by Don Madden
Printed in the U.S.A. All rights reserved.
10 9 8 7 6 5 4 3 2 1
First Edition

Library of Congress Cataloging-in-Publication Data
Sullivan, George, 1927–
    Pitcher.

    Summary: Explains the technical skills and
strategies it takes to be a pitcher.
    1. Pitching (Baseball)—Juvenile literature.
[1. Pitching (Baseball) 2. Baseball]
I. Madden, Don, 1927– ill. II. Title.
GV871.S8 1986   796.357'22   85-47939
ISBN 0-690-04538-7
ISBN 0-690-04539-5

ACKNOWLEDGEMENTS

Many people helped in the preparation of this book. The author is especially grateful to the Norshaft All Stars of Shaftsbury, Vermont, for their enthusiastic cooperation. Special thanks are due manager Noble Levesque and the many team members who posed for photographs. The author is also grateful to Francesca Kurti, T.L.C. Custom Labs, Aime LaMontagne and Bill Sullivan.

Contents

Pitcher

1

Before You Begin

PITCHER'S MOUND

In baseball, the pitcher is the most important player on the field. The pitcher is a team's offense.

It's the pitcher who puts the ball in play. It's the pitcher who decides where the ball is going to be thrown and how it is going to be thrown.

The batter is on the defensive. The batter must react to what the pitcher does. When the pitcher is good, the opposition finds it tough to score.

A team always has a chance to win. But if their pitcher has a bad day and gives up a bunch of runs, the team has to do some hard slugging to catch up.

What It Takes

To be an outstanding pitcher, you must have a smooth delivery and throw the ball hard with good control.

A player who is taller than average, with strong legs and good arm speed, has natural advantages when it comes to pitching. But you will find countless pitchers who don't fit that description. They're shorter than average and heavily built. But they make up their minds to succeed—and they do.

All pitchers require stamina. In Little League play, a game is six innings, with extra innings played when a tie results. (A game is nine innings in professional baseball.) In those six innings, a pitcher may throw as many as sixty or seventy pitches. That's not easy. It takes a strong arm and a strong body.

Warming Up

Be sure to protect your arm by warming up properly. Do the stretching exercises recommended by your coach. Also do some light running and other exercises, such as jumping jacks, to warm up your muscles and get your blood flowing before you pitch.

Your first warm-up throws should be over a short distance, 20 to 25 feet, about half the distance from the mound to home plate.

Slowly work your way up to the full distance—46 feet. Concentrate on control, not on speed. Take your time between throws.

Spend at least 15 to 20 minutes warming up.

Your Coach

When you're on the mound, you're always by yourself. Your performance depends pretty much on

you alone. But your coach will help to make your job easier.

The coach will help you to keep in shape. He will recommend what exercises and how much running to do. He'll set the length and type of each practice session.

Your coach will get to know you as a pitcher. If a flaw develops in your delivery, the coach should be able to spot it and tell you how to correct it.

During a game, the coach will watch you very carefully. It he thinks you're tiring, the coach will come to the mound and talk to you.

He may be trying to give you a breather or settle you down. Or he may simply want to discuss the next hitter with you.

The coach may decide, however, to take you out of the game in favor of a relief pitcher.

Naturally, you're going to feel bad. You may be convinced that you can get the next batter out. You may want to resist the coach's decision. But the coach may have noticed that you have lost some of your speed and control—or both. So go along with the coach. If you remain in the game, you could end up hurting the team.

Taking Care of Your Arm

You should never throw a baseball if you are sore or stiff in the shoulder or elbow.

After you've pitched in a game, do not throw again until your arm is rested and feels good.

If you've pitched four innings or less, you should rest your arm at least one full day.

If you've pitched more than four innings, you should rest at least three days.

Professional players must rest their arms, too. A major league pitcher, after a complete game, won't pitch again for four or five days.

When you are ready to pitch again, work slowly into peak form, gradually increasing your speed day by day.

Never pitch in a game after several days of not throwing. You can wreck your arm doing that.

During games, when you're on base and the weather is chilly, put on a jacket to keep your arm from getting stiff.

Working with weights can help to make your upper body stronger. Find out if your school has a weight-training program. Never lift weights without being supervised.

2

Delivering the Ball

No two pitchers use exactly the same motion in delivering the ball. Work to develop a delivery that feels natural to you and enables you to get the ball over the plate, pitch after pitch.

Types of Deliveries

There are three types of pitching deliveries: overhand, sidearm, and three-quarters.

Imagine the figure of a right-handed pitcher in front of a big clock. When the pitcher delivers the

11

Overhand delivery: top left
Sidearm delivery: top right
Three-quarters delivery: bottom right

ball straight overhand, his or her arm is positioned at 12 o'clock at the top of the delivery. The overhand delivery is like the serve in tennis.

In pitching with a sidearm motion, the arm delivers the ball at 9 o'clock.

With a three-quarters delivery, the arm comes through between 9 o'clock and 12 o'clock—at about 10 o'clock.

The overhand delivery is seldom seen. It makes throwing difficult.

The sidearm delivery isn't seen very often either. When you pitch sidearm, you're likely to be wild.

The three-quarters delivery is the one most pitchers use. It's the most natural of the three deliveries and it enables you to control the ball the best.

Getting Set

Face the batter squarely. Hold the ball in your pitching hand.

Then place the front part of your pivot foot (the right foot, if you're a right-hander) over the edge of the pitching rubber. Angle the foot out a bit so you'll be able to pivot easily.

Place your other foot—your stepping foot—a few inches behind the rubber.

Keep your back straight. Lean forward from the

waist. Keep your eyes on the catcher's mitt, your target. Peer in to get the signal from the catcher.

Winding Up

The windup, in which you rock back and forth on the mound, helps to get your weight moving toward the plate. That puts power into your delivery.

Swing your arms back, then forward, and up over your head. At the same time, shift your weight forward from your stepping foot to your pivot foot.

Then kick your stepping foot up. Don't kick too high because you can throw yourself off balance.

Step straight ahead, taking a giant step off the mound. Step directly toward the plate.

At the same time, pivot on the right foot. Turn the foot so your body turns, so your hip pocket briefly faces the batter.

Releasing the Ball

Just before your stepping foot touches down, bring your arm forward. Get the feeling you're driving your right shoulder toward your target. The arm should travel in a smooth and rhythmic arc.

The Follow-through

Even after the ball leaves your hand, your arm should continue moving. The hand should reach a point outside your left knee.

If you've delivered the ball correctly, you'll be bent deeply at the waist, your body square to the plate.

Your glove will be in front of your body. You're ready to dart in any direction to field a grounder.

3

Delivery with Runners on Base

You can't use your normal windup when there are runners on the bases. If you do, any runner can take a big lead and steal easily.

The Set Position

Instead, pitch from a set position. This enables you to keep an eye on the base runner. It also makes it easier for you to throw to a base. The runner is forced to stay closer to the bag.

In pitching from a set position, stand sideways,

your left shoulder toward the plate and your right foot in contact with the rubber. Hold the ball in both hands in front of your body.

Turn your head toward first and watch the runner out of the corner of your eye. Make him or her think you are about to throw over to the first baseman, whether or not you intend to do so.

While your foot is in contact with the rubber, whenever you make a move to first base or home plate, you must throw the ball there. Otherwise, you'll be guilty of a balk. Commit a balk and the runner is allowed to advance one base.

Delivering the Ball from the Set Position

In delivering the ball to the plate, you may first want to loosen your arms by stretching your hands up over your head. Then bring them down to chest or waist level. The arms must come to a complete stop before you deliver the ball.

To deliver the ball, simply shift your weight back to your right foot, then push off the rubber and stride forward with the left foot.

Don't kick your left leg as high as you do normally. Keep your foot closer to the ground. If you take the time to go through a normal windup and delivery, you'll be giving the runner a better chance to steal.

Runner on Third

Suppose you're pitching in a tight game. There's a runner on third with one out. As you go into your windup, the runner breaks for home.

What should you do?

Keep cool. Deliver the ball just as you would normally. But try to keep it low, targeting on the third base side of the plate. This gives the catcher a better chance of tagging the runner.

In most cases, the runner won't actually be stealing, but simply running partway down the line in an effort to get you nervous and make you throw wild.

Pitching Out

A pitchout is a pitch that is intentionally thrown wide of the plate (and that counts as a ball). It's just about impossible for the batter to hit. It enables the catcher to glove the ball easily and throw out a runner who is trying to steal second or third.

The catcher may also call for a pitchout when he wants to attempt to pick off a runner at first or third.

Anytime you're pitching out, your catcher will give you a target that is to the right or left of the plate. Throw a fastball for the target.

You can't let yourself be distracted by base runners. Your main job is to get the batter out. Before you start worrying about the runner, decide what pitch you're going to throw and where you're going to throw it. Then check the runner. Check your target. And pitch.

4

Grips

The number one pitch is the fastball. It usually travels arrow straight. But if you throw it fast enough, it will "move" a bit, probably rise slightly. It will be "live."

Fastball Grip

To throw a fastball, grip the ball with the second and third fingers resting across the seams where they are close together. The thumb should be underneath.

As the ball is thrown, snap the wrist and elbow forward. Allow the ball to roll off the end of the fingers. This makes the ball spin. The greater the spin, the more life the ball will have.

The Change-up

The second basic pitch is the change-up, also called the change of pace. Like the fastball, it travels in a straight line. But it is much slower.

Suppose you've pitched two or three fastballs in a row. The batter gets set, waiting for another, then in floats a change-up. It upsets the batter's timing. He or she is likely to swing before the ball arrives at the plate.

There are several different ways of gripping the ball when throwing a change-up. You can use the very same grip you use for your fastball. Or you can grip the ball well back in your palm, keeping the fingers raised.

What's important is that you do not snap the wrist as you deliver the ball. You simply release it by lifting your fingers. The ball must not spin.

To be effective, the change-up must be thrown with a delivery that looks exactly the same as your fastball delivery. If your delivery tips off the batter that the change-up is on its way, he or she is almost certain to hammer the ball hard.

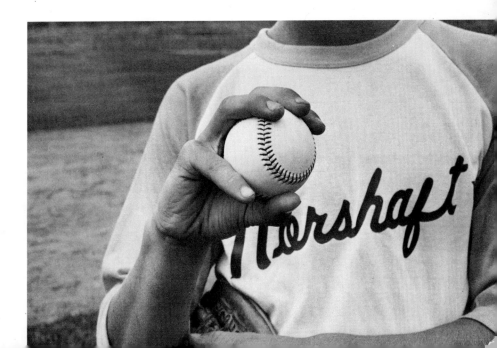

The Curve

After you've learned to throw a fastball and a change-up, you'll probably want to start working on a curve, a pitch that breaks down and away from the batter.

Be cautious about the curve, however. Throwing one can strain the arm's muscles, ligaments, and tendons, causing serious damage.

Don't even think about throwing a curve unless your coach says it's okay to do so.

Most pitchers throw a curve by gripping the ball with the middle finger along one of the seams. Your index finger should be almost touching the middle finger.

As you release the ball, snap your wrist all the way to the right. It's somewhat the same motion you use when turning a doorknob.

Let the ball roll off the index finger and the

CAUTION
DANGEROUS
CURVE

28

thumb. This makes the ball spin. The more it spins, the bigger the curve will be.

Professional players throw a variety of other pitches—the slider (a curve ball with a late break), sinker, and knuckleball. But these pitches, like the curve, really aren't necessary. If you have a good fastball and change-up, and are able to control them, you have all the weapons you need to be a successful pitcher.

Calling Pitches

You and the catcher must develop a signal system to indicate which pitch you're going to throw. One finger can mean a fastball; two fingers, a change-up. A fist can mean a pitchout.

After giving the sign, the catcher rises from a crouch to a semi-crouch position and gives a target with his or her mitt.

Besides signaling for pitches, the catcher plays other roles. If the catcher feels you're working too fast, he or she may slow you down by holding the ball longer between pitches.

When the batter bunts, follow the catcher's command. He or she may wave you away from the ball, shouting out, "I've got it!"

Or the catcher may shout, "It's yours! It's yours! Make the play!"

Learn to work closely with your catcher. You both should be in perfect agreement on how to pitch to the various hitters. You should know what to expect from one another in each defensive situation. You and your catcher should think as one person.

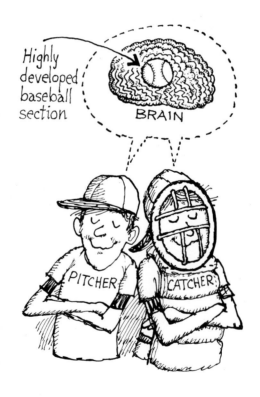

5

About Control

You can't be successful as a pitcher unless you throw accurately. That means having control.

There are two kinds of control. One type has to do with the ability to throw strikes, to make your fastball and change-up zip through the strike zone whenever you want.

The rule book defines the strike zone as the space over home plate between the batter's armpits and knees.

As this suggests, the strike zone varies in size, depending on the size of the batter. In the case of a

strike
zone

strike
zone

very tall batter, you have a large strike zone. But when you're facing a short batter who crouches, it shrinks. You have to be able to adjust to these variations.

You also have to be able to cope with batters who hit from the left side of the plate, as well as the right, with batters who crowd the plate and those who stand as far away as the rules permit, with batters who wave their bats as if to threaten you, and with those who stand quietly, almost like fenceposts.

No matter how well you're able to adjust, you're not going to be able to put the ball through the strike zone on every pitch. No pitcher can do that. But after you gain some experience, you should be able to put an average of three out of every four pitches through the strike zone.

The other type of control is more difficult to achieve. It is pinpoint control. It is the ability to throw the ball to a chosen spot within the strike zone—high or low, inside or outside.

some batter types
a pitcher has to cope with

How do you become a control pitcher?

First, you have to develop a smooth, effortless delivery with a good follow-through.

You also have to be consistent. Your delivery has to be exactly the same on every pitch. When you throw a particular pitch—a fastball, for example— you have to grip and release it the same way every time.

Control Problems

Suppose your pitches are coming in too high. This can be caused by taking too long a stride as you deliver the ball. Try shortening your stride.

If your pitches are missing the strike zone because they're too low, the opposite may be true—your stride may be too short. Make it a little longer.

The direction in which you stride is important, too. If, for example, your pitches are missing to the left of home plate, try striding a little farther to the right. If they're going wide to the right, stride more to the left.

Improving Your Control

Always throw to a target. Nothing is more important in improving control.

Even when you're playing catch with a friend, be

37

sure to throw to a target. Aim at your friend's belt buckle or one of the letters on his or her uniform.

Whenever you're warming up with a catcher, have the catcher give you a target with his or her mitt. Then aim for that.

Some pitchers get so used to throwing to their catcher during practice that when they face a batter in a game, it upsets them. They're so afraid they're going to hit the batter that they forget about their target. So when you're throwing to a catcher in practice, it's a good idea to have a batter stand at the plate, just as in a game, and take some practice cuts as you pitch.

During a game, instead of merely trying to put the ball over the plate, ask your catcher to set his or her mitt for high or low pitches, or inside or outside pitches. Then target on the mitt.

Practice Drill

You can also work to improve your control by chalking a strike zone on a wall and throwing a tennis ball or rubber ball toward it. Work with a full delivery, just as if you were pitching to a batter from the mound.

Once you're able to get the ball into the strike zone consistently, mark areas within the strike zone and try hitting each one.

It's great to know that you can put the ball exactly where you want it. When this happens, your confidence will zoom.

6

Pitching Strategy

Try extra hard to make your first pitch to each batter a strike. This gives you a big advantage over the hitter. If only one of your next four pitches finds the strike zone, the count will be 3–2. And 3–2 gives you an even chance of striking the batter out or walking him or her.

If your first pitch is a ball and the batter does not swing, things could be difficult for you. If the second pitch is also a ball, you're in a big hole. You must then put three of the next four pitches through the strike zone. It's hard to do that without

giving the batter a pitch that he or she is looking for, and a hit.

When you're behind the batter 3-0, the chances are good the batter is going to be letting the next pitch go by, hoping for a base on balls. But don't take this for granted and fire the ball across the heart of the plate. The batter can easily turn such a pitch into a base hit.

Expect the batter to be swinging. Throw to your catcher's target.

Moving the Ball Around

Suppose you've been successful in getting a particular hitter out a couple of times with fastballs low and away. The next time the hitter faces you, you have to figure he or she is going to be looking for that pitch. It might be best to pitch the hitter up and in. You can't let batters get used to your pitches.

Changing Your Pace

Another piece of strategy is to vary the amount of time between pitches. For example, if you feel the batter is itchy to hit, make him or her wait a little.

Waiting won't do the batter any good.

Some batters will try to use this strategy against you, taking extra time to get themselves set in the batter's box. Be prepared to wait them out.

Against a Choke-up Hitter

If a hitter chokes up on the bat, it's a pretty good tip-off that he or she is merely going to try to make contact with the ball, maybe try to slap it over an infielder's head.

Keep the ball down against a hitter who chokes up. This causes such a batter to hit low and ground out.

Against a Weak Hitter

Don't get careless when facing a hitter you look upon as an easy out. Bear down just as if you're up against a powerful slugger.

It's never a good idea to throw a change-up to a weak batter. If you do, duck. Weak hitters feast on change-ups, because slow pitches are easiest for them to hit.

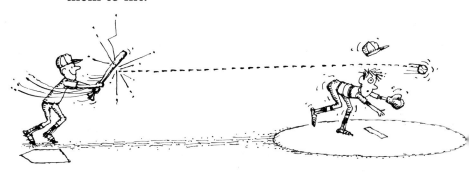

Other Strategies

• As a general rule, keep your pitches below the batter's waist. Pitches low in the strike zone are more difficult to hit.

• When you expect the batter is going to be trying to bunt, throw a high, inside fastball. Almost any pitch that's high and inside is tough to bunt.

• When a right-handed batter is trying to hit the ball behind the runner on first (to the right side of the infield), keep the ball low and away. Most rightie batters find it easier to hit an inside pitch when trying to poke the ball to the right side.

• Suppose you're facing a powerful pull hitter, a batter who hits the ball to the field on the same side of the plate as he or she stands. (A right-handed batter stands on the left side of home plate and "pulls" the ball to left field.)

A pull hitter is likely to be waiting to take advantage of an outside pitch. So try an inside letter-high fastball.

Hang In There

When you're pitching and your team falls behind, don't give up. Pitch just as if the game were close and you were protecting a slim lead. You can never tell what is going to happen. As Hall-of-Famer Yogi Berra once said, "The game isn't over till it's over." Your team can always come back and score a bushel of runs. So don't let up.

7

Fielding Your Position

Remember, you're not only a pitcher, you're an infielder, too. You must be alert to field ground balls, throw to bases, and even make putouts at first base.

Let's suppose there are runners on first and second. There are two outs. The hitter smashes a ground ball toward the mound. You field it cleanly. You throw to first base and nail the runner.

You could have thrown to second base or third and made a force out. But throwing to first was the correct play. The first baseman is used to covering

the base in such situations, and you know the first baseman is going to be there.

You followed the general rule that covers most fielding plays: *Make the easiest play possible.*

But sometimes the pitcher is involved in plays that are a bit unusual. The general rule doesn't apply. Let's look at some of these.

Covering First

Suppose there are no outs and the bases are empty. The batter slashes a high bouncer to your left. The first baseman gloves the ball between first and second base.

Since the runner is going to reach first base before the first baseman, it's up to you to break for first base and get there before the runner. The first baseman will toss the ball to you. Catch it on the run as you approach the base. Then tag the base with your right foot.

This play is easy to execute as long as you get into position fast, arriving at first base ahead of the runner. Don't wait at the mound to see how the play is unfolding. Anytime the ball is hit on the ground to your left and the play is at first base, dash for the base. As you near it, turn toward the first baseman and get ready to take the toss on the run.

After fielding the ball, the first baseman may wave you out of the way and make the play. That's fine. What's important is to be there in case you're needed.

Backing Up

Or suppose this situation arises: There is a runner on second with no outs. The hitter drives one of your pitches over second base into center field. The center fielder scoops up the ball on one bounce. The runner from second is racing around third and heading for home.

What should you be doing?

It's likely there's going to be a play at home. It's your job to back up the catcher. If the ball should get away from the catcher, you can retrieve it and prevent the runner from second from scoring.

You should also cover home plate anytime there is a runner on second or third base and you uncork a wild pitch. The catcher is going to whip off his or her mask and tear after the ball. You should charge for the plate. Yell to the catcher to let him or her know you're there. Then the catcher won't have to look for you and can quickly turn and throw.

You have to react quickly because you must get to the plate ahead of the runner. You should also cover the plate when there is a runner on second or third and the catcher is guilty of a passed ball—that is, he or she fails to stop one of your pitches.

Let's look at one other situation. There is a runner on first base with no outs. The batter lashes a single into right field. The runner on first rounds second base and heads for third.

The right fielder fires the ball to the third baseman in an attempt to nail the runner trying to go from first to third.

Your job is to back up the third baseman in case he or she bobbles the throw from the right fielder. If this should happen, you can retrieve the ball and prevent the runner from scoring.

A pitcher can never be a spectator, standing around and watching the game. There's always a job for you to do.

8

Winning and Losing

You're not going to win every game, or lose every one. You're likely to chalk up about the same number of wins as losses.

When you do win, enjoy it with your team. You've all earned it. Praise any of your teammates who contributed to the victory. Give the losing players a pat on the back, too.

When you lose, don't make excuses, such as blaming the umpire. Umpires don't lose or win games. Players do.

Don't blame your teammates, either. You can't,

for example, let an error by a teammate upset you.

All you want your teammates to do is try their hardest, to give one hundred percent. An error by a player who is trying should never bother you.

If you make an error, don't let it affect your pitching. Bear down. Learn from your mistakes.

Sure, it's important whether you win or lose. But it's more important to enjoy yourself, to have fun.